CURIOUS PEARL
SCIENCE GIRL

CURIOUS PEARL
DIVES INTO WEATHER

by Eric Braun

illustrated by Anthony Lewis

raintree
a Capstone company — publishers for children

Curious Pearl here!
Do you like science?

I certainly do! I have all sorts of fun tools to help me observe and investigate, but my favourite tool is my science notebook. That's where I write down questions and facts that help me learn more about science. Would you like to join me on my science adventures? You're in for a special surprise!

Aaaaaah, feel the sun on your skin and the sand in your toes. There's no better place than the beach to read a science book.

"Come on, Pearl," said my friend Sabina. "Let's get in the water!"

"Can I finish this chapter first?" I asked. "I'm reading about weather."

"The weather is fantastic right now!" Sabina said. "Why read about it when we can enjoy it?"

"I'm not reading about today's weather," I said. "I'm reading about everything that makes up weather."

"What makes up weather?" asked Sabina. "Weather is weather."

I showed Sabina a page in my book. "Weather is made up of a combination of things: sunlight, wind, precipitation and temperature. Wherever you are, those elements are all present in some form.

They work together and give us different weather conditions."

"Well, they must be working together well today," Sabina said. "This weather is perfect!"

"They are for now!" I said. "But the elements can change, which will cause the weather to change. Sometimes very quickly."

As we waded into the water, the sun reflected off the surface and into our eyes.

"Wow, it's bright," Sabina said.

"That's because there aren't any clouds," I said. "Clouds determine how much sunlight we see. If there are lots of clouds, it's not so bright."

"Actually, I can see a few clouds," Sabina said. She pointed to the horizon.

"Eureka! That's a cirrus cloud!" I said.

"What's a serious cloud?" Sabina asked.

"Not serious. Cirrus is a type of cloud. There are four main types of clouds."

I took my notebook out of my bag to show her the four types of clouds. What? Don't you keep a notebook with you at all times?

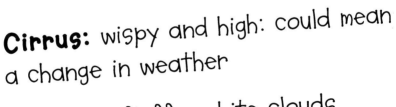

Cirrus: wispy and high: could mean a change in weather

Cumulus: fluffy, white clouds usually seen on a nice day

Stratus: low, dark layer of cloud that can cover most of the sky (not very sunny!)

Nimbus: dark grey cloud usually holding rain

"Wind is part of weather," I said. "It can be still, breezy or windy. Or really windy."

"Like that time when my homework got caught by the wind," Sabina said. "Remember?"

"We had to chase it all the way down the street," I giggled.

"I wonder why some days it's windy, and other days it's not," Sabina said.

"Let's look it up!" I said. We ran back to look in my weather book.

Cool air makes high air pressure, and warm air makes low air pressure. Warm air rises, and cold air falls. When the two meet, the differences in pressure make wind!

"This is my favourite weather," Sabina said. "Hot!"

"Temperature is another part of weather," I told her. "Temperature is the measure of how cold or hot it is. It's expressed as a number of degrees." I turned the pages in my weather book to the part about temperature. I made a note in my science notebook.

Temperature is measured on two main scales, Celsius and Fahrenheit. They both tell us the same thing, just using different numbers. For example, water freezes at 0 degrees Celsius, but that's 32 degrees Fahrenheit.

"Okay," Sabina said. "So there are clouds and sun. There's wind. And there's temperature. I've forgotten – what's the last part of weather?"

"Precipitation," I said. "That's how much rain or snow is falling."

"I'm glad it's not raining or snowing today," Sabina said.

I looked out at the grey cloud on the horizon. "Remember," I said, "weather can change."

"Why do you want to study weather anyway?" Sabina asked.

"Well, my book says that people measure all the parts of weather so they can notice patterns over time. That way they can predict what the weather might be like in different places at different times," I said.

"All right," Sabina said. "You said that weather can change. But I still don't get why anyone bothers studying it. We can't change it."

"No," I said. "But knowing ahead of time can be helpful. If you know what type of weather is likely to come, you can make plans for the future. You'd know not to go camping when the weather is likely to be cold and wet."

Just then, my little brother Peter's Frisbee landed in the water by us, so I dived down to get it. When I came back up, I threw it back to shore. It landed next to Dad's umbrella.

"Why has your dad got an umbrella?" Sabina asked. "It's not raining."

"It's not raining now, but remember what I said about using weather patterns to predict weather? Dad and I looked at the weather report on the internet this morning. The website said it might rain today."

Sabina looked up at the clouds she'd seen earlier. "They are getting closer and darker," she said.

"Those are nimbus clouds," I said. "They carry rain."

"Let's get out of here," Sabina said. "I don't want to get rained on."

We got to the beach just in time. It started pouring!

At home, we dried off, and started talking about moving to somewhere with a different climate. "Climate is the range of weather that is typical to an area," I said.

"Could we live in a climate that doesn't have much rain?" Sabina asked.

"Of course," I said. "The desert doesn't have much rain. But the temperature gets very hot. You might not like that."

"Hmmm . . . what other types of climates are there?" asked Sabina.

I grabbed my trusty science notebook to make a list of the five main types of climates.

Tropical: hot and humid; close to the equator

Arid: dry, like in deserts

Temperate: summers are hot and dry, winters are cool and wet

Continental: long, cold winters and short, hot summers

Polar: very cold for long periods of time

Dad reached over to grab our wet towels. "Every climate has certain types of severe weather," he added.

"Severe weather?" Peter asked. "You mean like hurricanes?"

"Yep," Dad said. "But we won't get hurricanes here because the sea isn't warm enough. We know that hurricanes are not part of our climate. But we can get severe storms and floods."

"Oh, no!" Peter said.

"Don't worry," I said. "We won't have a flood today. If something like that was coming, scientists would warn us. That's another reason why they study weather – so that communities can be ready if severe weather comes."

Sabina and I did some research online and made a list of a few types of severe weather.

Thunderstorm: rain storm with lightning and thunder; sometimes there's hail or severe wind

Tornado: narrow, violent column of twisting air

Flood: when too much water flows onto land that is ordinarily dry

Hail: when thunderstorms produce frozen balls of ice

Sabina and I turned on the TV to watch the weather forecast for tomorrow. It was good news. Another hot, sunny day means another day at the beach!

Meanwhile, Sabina had brought back some colourful rocks from our day out. We decided that a rainy day is a good excuse to do something different: make pet rocks.

Make wind

Wind is created when hot air rises. Try this simple experiment to see how it works.

Here's what you need:

- Sheet of paper
- Pen or pencil
- Scissors
- Drawing pin
- Short length of thread
- Coat hanger
- Source of heat, such as a radiator or lamp turned upwards

Steps:

1. Draw a spiral on the sheet of paper and cut it out.

2. Use the drawing pin to poke a hole in the centre.

3. Push the thread through the hole and tie a knot.

4. Tie the other end of the thread to the coat hanger.

5. Holding the hanger, dangle your spiral a few centimetres above the heat source and wait.

Did the spiral start to spin? The reason is that the warm air rising from the heat source pushes it. This is the same way wind happens. Warm air rises, causing cooler air to be pulled in to take its place.

GLOSSARY

climate range of weather that is likely in a particular area

cloud mass of water in the sky

forecast prediction about the weather

precipitation water that falls from the sky, such as rain or snow

severe weather dangerous weather that may cause damage, disruption or loss of life

temperature how hot or cold something is as measured in degrees

wind moving air

READ MORE

Mapping the Land and Weather (Let's Get Mapping!), Melanie Waldron (Raintree, 2014)

Weather (Nature Explorers), DK (DK Children, 2017)

Weather Infographics, Chris Oxlade (Raintree, 2015)

WEBSITES

www.bbc.co.uk/guides/zsqnfg8
Learn more about desert habitats and life without much rain.

www.dkfindout.com/uk/earth/weather/weather-forecasting
Find out more about how scientists forecast the weather.

COMPREHENSION QUESTIONS

Describe the climate where you live. Make sure you mention weather for every season. What types of severe weather do you get?

What is an activity you've done or a trip you've taken that depended on the weather? How did you plan for this activity?

What is your favourite weather? Describe what all the parts of weather are like.

BOOKS IN THIS SERIES

INDEX

Thanks to our advisor for his expertise, research and advice:
Paul Ohmann, PhD.

Raintree is an imprint of Capstone Global Library Limited,
a company incorporated in England and Wales having its
registered office at 264 Banbury Road, Oxford, OX2 7DY –
Registered company number: 6695582

www.raintree.co.uk
myorders@raintree.co.uk

Text © Capstone Global Library Limited 2019
The moral rights of the proprietor have been asserted.

All rights reserved. No part of this publication may be
reproduced in any form or by any means (including photocopying
or storing it in any medium by electronic means and whether
or not transiently or incidentally to some other use of this
publication) without the written permission of the copyright
owner, except in accordance with the provisions of the
Copyright, Designs and Patents Act 1988 or under the terms of a
licence issued by the Copyright Licensing Agency, Barnard's Inn,
86 Fetter Lane, London, EC4A 1EN (www.cla.co.uk). Applications
for the copyright owner's written permission should be
addressed to the publisher.

Designed by Ted Williams and Nathan Gassman
Cover illustrated by Stephanie Dehennin
The illustrations in the book were digitally produced.
Original illustrations © Capstone Global Library Limited 2019
Production by Tori Abraham
Originated by Capstone Global Library Ltd
Printed and bound in India

ISBN 978 1 4747 6322 6

British Library Cataloguing in Publication Data
A full catalogue record for this book is available from the British
Library.

Every effort has been made to contact copyright holders of
material reproduced in this book. Any omissions will be rectified
in subsequent printings if notice is given to the publisher.

All the internet addresses (URLs) given in this book were valid at
the time of going to press. However, due to the dynamic nature
of the internet, some addresses may have changed, or sites may
have changed or ceased to exist since publication. While the
author and publisher regret any inconvenience this may cause
readers, no responsibility for any such changes can be accepted
by either the author or the publisher

Printed and bound in the United Kingdom.